THE

GLORIOUS

GOD

My Fight Against Epilepsy

BY GEMIRACLE IVEY

AuthorHouse™
1663 Liberty Drive
Bloomington, IN 47403
www.authorhouse.com
Phone: 833-262-8899

Because of the dynamic nature of the Internet, any web addresses or links contained in this book may have changed
since publication and may no longer be valid. The views expressed in this work are solely those of the author and do
not necessarily reflect the views of the publisher, and the publisher hereby disclaims any responsibility for them.

Any people depicted in stock imagery provided by Getty Images are models,
and such images are being used for illustrative purposes only.
Certain stock imagery © Getty Images.

This book is printed on acid-free paper.

ISBN: 979-8-8230-3023-6 (sc)
979-8-8230-3024-3 (e)

Library of Congress Control Number: 2024915101

Print information available on the last page.

Published by AuthorHouse 07/18/2024

authorHOUSE®

Table of Contents

THE GLORIOUS GOD

In the depths of despair, as relentless seizures wracked my body, I turned to the only refuge I had left: my faith in God. With every surge of electricity coursing through my brain, I clung to the belief that my Glorious God held the power to heal and restore. Through countless sleepless nights and moments of doubt, I poured out my heart in fervent prayer, seeking His guidance and strength. As I surrendered my life to His will, a flicker of hope began to ignite within me. And so, in the darkest hours, relying solely on my God, I triumphed over the relentless grip of epilepsy. This is my story, a testament to the transformative power of prayer and the unwavering love of a God who never abandoned me in my greatest need. In sharing it, I seek to inspire others to embrace the power of faith, even in the face of adversity, knowing that the Glorious God is always with us, offering hope and healing in our darkest hours.

CHAPTER ONE

BLESSINGS

I want to share with you all how I overcame my fight with epilepsy. It all started when I was a young child and was first diagnosed with seizures. The first signs were blank out spells where I would pass out unexpectedly. As I grew older, the seizures became more frequent and intense, making it difficult for me to focus in a regular classroom setting.

The seizures not only affected my ability to learn, but they also frightened my peers. I remember the looks of concern and fear on their faces as I would have a seizure. The school suggested placing me in special education classes, but my parents were against it. They believed in my abilities and insisted that my seizures were not affecting my learning.

Despite their support, the seizures continued to disrupt my life. My mom was constantly being called to the school to pick me up after an episode. It was frustrating and demoralizing, and I began to lose hope. That's when I turned to my faith for strength.

I remember praying to my Glorious God for a supernatural healing. I prayed fervently, asking for the seizures to leave my body. But the healing didn't come instantly. Instead, I endured many trials and tribulations as I continued to battle epilepsy.

Through it all, I remained determined to overcome this obstacle in my life. Epilepsy was not only ruining my education, but it was also taking a toll on my self-esteem. I felt like I was different from everyone else, like I didn't fit in.

However, It was then I recalled being in kindergarten when I got in my first fight because a child laughed at me when I had a seizure inside the classroom. They laughed when I came out of my seizure, saying I shook like a robot. It was a confusing and hurtful experience for me, as I didn't fully understand what was happening to my body during those moments.

I had been diagnosed with epilepsy at a young age, so seizures were not something new to me. However, it was difficult to deal with the reactions of others, especially when they were hurtful or made fun of me. I found myself getting into a lot of fights due to my condition, as I tried to defend myself from the mockery and ignorance of my peers.

But everything changed when I entered the second grade. I was placed in a class with a kind and understanding teacher who took the time to learn about epilepsy and how to support me. She treated me like her own child, making sure I felt safe and included in the classroom. With her help, I began to feel more accepted and supported by my classmates as well.

However, my seizures continued to be a challenge for me academically. They often prevented me from focusing and understanding my assignments, causing me to fall behind in my schoolwork. My neurologist prescribed medication to help me focus in class, but it didn't provide much relief. I continued to struggle, feeling frustrated and overwhelmed by my condition.

Eventually, my mom made the difficult decision to homeschool me during my third and fourth grade years. It was a big adjustment for both of us, as we had to navigate the world of online schooling together. My mom worked a full-time job, so there were days when she had to take me to work with her because there was nowhere else for me to go.

I remember sitting in my mom's office, trying to focus on my lessons while she worked diligently on her computer. It was a challenging time for us, but we made the best of it. I could see the stress and exhaustion in my mom's eyes as she juggled work and caring for me, and I prayed to my Glorious God to help alleviate some of that burden from her.

When it was time for me to return to regular school in fifth grade, I was filled with mixed emotions. I was excited to be back in a traditional classroom setting, but I was also nervous about how my classmates would react to my condition. However, with the support of my mom and my newfound confidence, I faced the challenges head- on.

CHAPTER TWO

DRIVEN & DETERMINED

As I prepared to enter high school, I reflected on the challenges I had faced throughout my middle school years. Living with epilepsy had been difficult, with regular seizures disrupting my daily life. Despite this, I remained determined to not let it hold me back. With the support of my family and faith in God, I faced each day with strength and resilience.

High school brought a new set of challenges, with a larger campus and more demanding coursework. I found myself feeling both excited and nervous as I navigated the hallways, trying to locate my classes in a sea of unfamiliar faces. However, I was not alone in this journey. I had my faith as my anchor, guiding me through the ups and downs of high school life.

Joining the choir and various school clubs allowed me to explore my interests and make new friends. I threw myself into my studies, determined to excel academically despite the obstacles I had faced in the past. I was independent and driven, always pushing myself to reach new heights. My faith in God only strengthened as I saw His hand guiding me through each challenge and triumph.

However, as I turned sixteen, I made a decision that would change my life forever. During a visit to my neurologist, I made the bold choice to stop taking my epilepsy medications. I informed the doctor that I believed in the healing power of God and no longer needed the medication to control my seizures. My mother stood by my side, her unwavering support giving me the courage to take this leap of faith.

Leaving the neurologist's office, I felt a sense of liberation. I had put my trust in God to heal my body, and I believed with all my heart that He would see me through. And indeed, as days turned into weeks, I realized that the seizures were gone. I was free from the burden that had weighed me down for so long, able to embrace my high school journey with newfound joy and freedom.

It was the summer of 2018, and I had just graduated from high school. The feeling of accomplishment and pride overwhelmed me as I walked across the stage to receive my diploma. Surrounded by my family and friends, I knew that this day was the result of hard work and determination.

Despite the challenges I faced due to my epilepsy, I never let it hold me back. With the support of my loved ones and my unwavering faith in God, I was able to overcome any obstacles that came my way. I celebrated my graduation with a heart full of gratitude, giving all the glory to the One who had sustained me through it all.

As I looked towards the future, I knew that I wanted to continue my education and pursue my dreams. I enrolled in college with a clear goal in mind - to obtain a degree in accounting. My parents had worked hard to build their company, and I wanted to be able to support them by helping to run the business.

Now, as I navigate through my college courses and prepare for my future career, I am filled with a sense of excitement and purpose. I am determined to make the most of this opportunity and to use my skills and knowledge to contribute to my family's success.

I may have won the battle against epilepsy, but the real victory lies in the life that I am now able to lead. I am grateful for every moment, every opportunity, and every blessing that has come my way. And I know that with dedication, persistence, and faith, I will continue to achieve great things in the future.

As I look back on my life, I am filled with gratitude for the strength and resilience that God instilled in me. My faith in Him carried me through the darkest moments and celebrated with me in the brightest. I learned the power of perseverance and the importance of trusting in something greater than myself.

With each passing day, my relationship with God deepened, and I found myself leaning on Him for guidance and support in all aspects of my life. I am grateful for the challenges I faced, as they shaped me into the person I am today – a strong, independent individual who believes in the power of faith and the miracles it can bring.

As I prepare to embark on the next chapter of my life, I do so with a heart full of thankfulness and a spirit brimming with hope. I know that whatever challenges come my way, I have the strength and faith to overcome them. And I will forever be grateful for the miraculous healing that God bestowed upon me, allowing me to live my life to the fullest without the interference of epilepsy.

Epilepsy has taught me to love myself and to never take life for granted. It has shown me that every moment is precious and should be treasured. Despite the challenges it brings, I have learned to appreciate the beauty of life in a whole new way.

My Glorious God is always by my side, giving me strength and courage to face whatever comes my way. I know that no matter how hard life becomes, I am never alone. My faith in Him is my rock, my fortress in times of trouble.

Epilepsy may try to knock me down, but it has only made me stronger. It has taught me resilience and perseverance in the face of adversity. With God as my protector, I can stand firm against the trials and tribulations that come my way.

I am grateful for the lessons that epilepsy has taught me. It has shown me the power of faith and the importance of self-love. Despite the challenges, I know that my Glorious God will always be with me.

CHAPTER THREE

GOD'S LOVE

I want to take a moment to give praise to my Glorious God, who has been so good to me throughout my life. His love is truly unconditional and everlasting, guiding me through both joyful moments and challenging times. From a young age, I was diagnosed with epilepsy, a condition that brought fear and uncertainty into my life. However, through God's grace, I have been able to overcome this obstacle and thrive as a college student pursuing a degree in accounting.

God's love knows no bounds and He desires for us to walk in obedience. While it may be difficult at times, I have found that it is possible to follow His commandments and experience the blessings that come with it. Deuteronomy 28:1 speaks of the great blessings that await those who remain obedient to God, and I have witnessed these blessings firsthand in my own life.

Learning to love others unconditionally and to forgive those who have wronged me has been a transformative experience on my spiritual journey. By embracing these principles, I have seen how my relationship with God has deepened and how His love has shaped my interactions with those around me. Through every trial and tribulation, I have held onto the belief that my Glorious God has a plan for me, one that is filled with purpose and hope.

Despite the challenges that epilepsy has presented in my life, I have learned to trust in God's goodness and His faithfulness. Instead of allowing anger and frustration to consume me during moments of physical weakness, I have turned to God for strength and resilience. His unwavering love has been a source of comfort and peace during the most difficult times, reminding me that I am never alone in my struggles.

As I look towards the future and the prospect of graduating with my accounting degree, I am filled with gratitude for the ways in which God has guided me along this path. His hand has been evident in every success and every setback, showing me that His plans for me are greater than I could ever imagine. I am inspired to continue living in obedience to God's will, knowing that He will continue to shower me with His blessings and grace.

In conclusion, I want to thank my Glorious God for His unfailing love and His endless mercies. Through His guidance and support, I have been able to overcome obstacles and achieve my goals. I hold onto the promise that God withholds no good thing from those who walk uprightly, and I am confident that His plans for me are filled with prosperity and joy. My heart overflows with gratitude for the love and goodness of my Glorious God, who has been my rock and my salvation throughout every season of my life.

I am filled with gratitude for the unwavering support of my parents. They had always been there for me, cheering me on through every triumph and setback. But it was not just their love and encouragement that inspired me, it was also their unwavering faith in God.

Living with epilepsy had not been easy. The seizures were unpredictable and often left me feeling helpless. But through it all, my parents stood by my side, holding me up when I felt like I could not go on. And in those moments of darkness, it was their love that shone the brightest.

I will never forget the look of fear and helplessness in my mother's eyes when she saw me having a seizure. It tore at my heart to see her in such pain, but she never wavered in her belief that God would heal me. And it was that faith that kept me going, that gave me the strength to push through the toughest of days.

Through it all, I learned to love and appreciate my parents in a way I never thought possible. They were my rocks, my pillars of strength, and I knew that as long as they, and most of all, my Glorious God were by my side, I could overcome anything. And for that, I will be forever grateful.

CHAPTER FOUR

BELIEVE

I have always believed in the power of God to do the unthinkable. Growing up, my mom instilled in me the importance of faith and trusting in God's plan for my life. She would always remind me that God's love is enduring and everlasting and that He wants us to live in peace and abundance.

One particular verse from the Bible that someone quoted to her was Deuteronomy 28:1, which says, "If you fully obey the Lord your God and carefully follow all his commands I give you today, the Lord your God will set you high above all the nations on earth." This verse served as a constant reminder to me that it is possible to obey all of God's commands, and that when we trust and believe in God, He will pour out His blessings upon us.

I remember a time when my faith in God was put to the test. As I aforementioned stated, After being diagnosed with epilepsy at a young age, I struggled with debilitating seizures that would often leave me feeling helpless and defeated. I tried various medications and treatments, but nothing seemed to work. It was during this difficult time that my mom encouraged me to lean on my faith and trust in God's healing power.

I began to pray fervently, asking God to heal me and restore my health. I immersed myself in the Bible, seeking comfort and guidance in His words. Slowly but surely, I started to see a change in my condition. The seizures became less frequent, and my overall health began to improve.

As my faith in God grew stronger, so did my belief in His ability to do the impossible. I started to live each day as if it were my last, cherishing every moment and embracing the blessings that God had bestowed upon me. I no longer lived in fear of the unknown, but rather in confidence that God was in control and had a plan for my life.

And true to His word, God began to work miracles in my life. The seizures disappeared completely, and I was able to live a life free from the constraints of my illness. I knew that it was only through God's grace and mercy that I had been healed, and I was forever grateful for His love and compassion.

I realized then that when we honor God and keep His commandments, He truly does exhale us above all nations. He opens the windows of Heaven and pours out blessings, favor, and honor upon us. God's love knows no bounds, and His power is limitless. I learned that with faith, all things are possible and that God can do anything except fail.

As I look back on my journey of faith and healing, I am reminded of the words of Hebrews 11:6, which says, "And without faith, it is impossible to please God." I am grateful for the unwavering faith that my mom instilled in me, and for the incredible miracles that God has worked in my life.

I now live each day with a renewed sense of purpose and gratitude, knowing that God's love is enduring and His power is unmatched. I continue to trust in His plan for my life, believing that He can do the unthinkable and that He will never fail me. And I am filled with hope and joy, knowing that I serve a Glorious God who is always faithful and true.

CHAPTER FIVE

TRUST

G rowing up, I was diagnosed with epilepsy at a young age. The seizures were unpredictable and often left me feeling scared and helpless. I remember feeling like my life was constantly overshadowed by this condition, and I longed for a way to be free from it.

As I grew older, I found solace in my faith. I turned to God in prayer, asking Him to deliver me from epilepsy and to guide me towards a path of healing. I knew that trusting in God's plan for my life was the only way I could find peace and hope amidst the chaos of my medical condition.

My mom was my rock during those difficult times. She would often remind me to always trust in our Glorious God and that He would provide and release miracles and blessings into my life in due season. Her words gave me the strength to hold on to my faith, even when it seemed like my prayers were going unanswered.

One day, during a particularly challenging season of my life, I felt a sense of peace wash over me. It was as if God was telling me to trust

Him completely and to surrender my fears and doubts. And so, I did. I let go of my worries and put my faith in God's will for my life.

And then, something incredible happened. I began to notice small changes in my health. The frequency of my seizures decreased, and I was able to go longer periods of time without experiencing any episodes. It was as if God was working behind the scenes, orchestrating a miraculous transformation within me.

I continued to trust in God's plan for my life, and as I did, doors of opportunity began to open before me. I was able to pursue my passions and dreams with a newfound sense of confidence and determination. God's love and guidance propelled me forward, leading me towards a brighter future filled with hope and promise.

As time passed, I realized that God's timing is perfect. He knows what is best for us, and when we trust and obey His word, He will deliver us from our trials and lead us towards a path of abundance and grace. My faith in God had brought forth miracles and blessings that I never thought possible.

I am now living a life free from epilepsy, and I am filled with gratitude and awe for the incredible ways in which God has worked in my life. I have learned to always trust in God to provide for me and to trust His will for my life. When we have faith like a mustard seed and trust Him wholeheartedly, He will do exceedingly above all that we can ask or think.

In every season of our lives, there is a time for miracles and blessings to unfold. And when we trust in our Glorious God, He will release His divine favor and grace upon us, guiding us towards a future filled with abundance and purpose. Trust in Him, for He is faithful and His promises never fail.

About the Author

I am a 2018 high school graduate and a 2021 college graduate with a Business certificate in accounting. In addition to my studies, I also work as a tax preparer in my family's tax business. It's a challenging job, but I enjoy the opportunity to help others navigate the complicated world of taxes.

One thing that sets me apart from many of my peers is that I am an epilepsy survivor. Dealing with this condition has taught me resilience and perseverance, qualities that have served me well in both my academic and professional pursuits.

In my free time, I enjoy writing. Whether it's journaling about my experiences or creating my life journey stories, I find solace in putting pen to paper. I also find great joy in serving my Glorious God, whose presence has been a source of strength and comfort throughout my journey.

As I continue on my path toward obtaining my business degree, I am grateful for the opportunities that lie ahead. I know that with dedication and determination, I can achieve my goals and make a positive impact in both my career and my community. This is my first published book.

2005

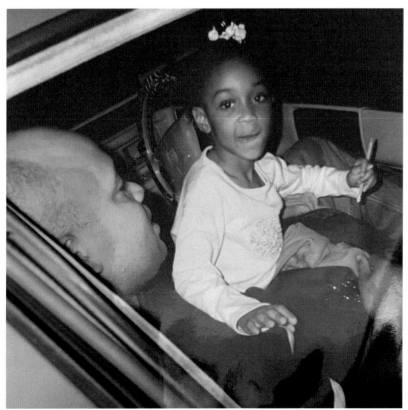

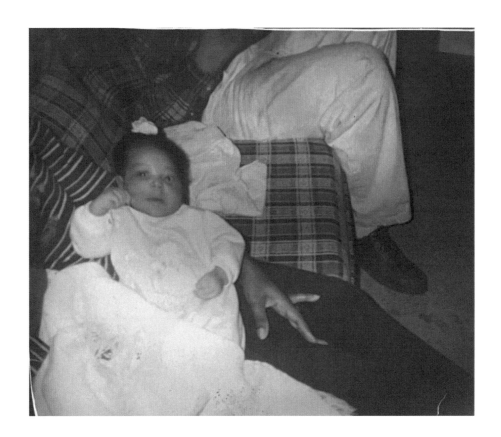

Printed in the United States
by Baker & Taylor Publisher Services